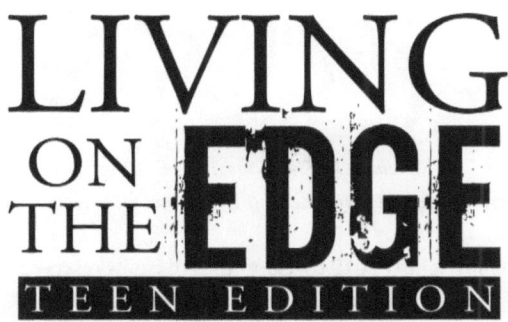

HOW TO FIGHT AND WIN THE BATTLE FOR YOUR MIND AND HEART

GARY ROE

Living On The Edge Teen Edition
How to fight and win the battle for your mind and heart

Copyright © 2019 by Gary Roe All rights reserved.
First Edition: 2019

ISBN: 978-1-950382-15-6

Cover and Formatting: Streetlight Graphics

No part of this book may be reproduced, scanned, or distributed in any printed or electronic form without permission. Please do not participate in or encourage piracy of copyrighted materials in violation of the author's rights. Thank you for respecting the hard work of this author.

The author is not engaged in rendering medical or psychological services, and this book is not intended as a guide to diagnose or treat medical or psychological problems. If you require medical, psychological, or other expert assistance, please seek the services of your own physician or licensed professional counselor.

TABLE OF CONTENTS

We're All Living On The Edge 1

Hit And Wounded 3

Self-Harming And Suicidal Thoughts 5

Living On A Different Kind Of Edge 11

Replacing Lies With The Truth 13

The Four-Step Challenge 23

One Last Thing: 27

Rachel's Story 29

An Urgent Request 31

About The Author 33

Keep Going! 35

WE'RE ALL LIVING ON THE EDGE

LET'S BE HONEST. OUR WORLD is less than terrific. It is harsh. Life is tough.

Bad stuff happens. To me. To you. To those we love and care about.

We live on the edge, wondering what's coming next. We become desperate. Sometimes we even climb over others to get what good we can.

We're scared, anxious, angry, and sad.

We try, but we're never good enough. We're never smart enough. We're never attractive enough.

We're more connected than ever but feel incredibly alone.

No one understands. No one gets it.

We wear masks. We try to be someone else. We live lies. We exist in fight-or-flight mode.

You've felt this.

Maybe you're feeling it now.

We're on a downward spiral.

Maybe you're on a downward spiral.

There is a fierce battle going on in your mind. Your heart is at stake.

So, what do we do about this?

What will *you* do about this?

One option is to do nothing. Get up each day, have the same thoughts and live the same way and hope for different results.

That's what most of us do.

Another option is to wait for someone else to do something. Surely someone else will act and change our lives for the better.

This "better" we chase, however, is a fantasy.

Yet, again, we do this.

We do nothing. We wait for others to do something. We expect things to be magically different.

The definition of insanity is doing the same thing over and over and expecting different results. By this definition, the world is insane. All of us are…at least a little bit.

So, what can you do?

Do things differently. This begins with learning to think differently.

How do you do that?

HIT AND WOUNDED

We've all been wounded. Many of us are limping badly. Some of us are nearly paralyzed.

The hits of life shape us. If we get hit enough, the pain gets our attention and can begin to take over.

Our wounds come with messages attached to them.

"You don't matter."

"You're worthless."

"You're ugly."

"You're stupid."

"You're damaged."

"You'll never be enough."

These messages pile up. Soon we begin hearing them in our own voices.

"I don't matter. I'm worthless."

"I'm ugly. I'm stupid."

"I'm damaged. I'll never be enough."

And then comes the clincher.

"It will always be this way."

Then comes the apathy.

"Whatever."

Wounds influence our thoughts and alter our thinking. Life itself can seem dark and sad.

No wonder many of us begin to wonder if life is worth it.

GARY ROE

> **Living life on the edge of your seat
> vs.
> walking along the edge of a cliff.
> Knowing the difference is important.**

SELF-HARMING AND SUICIDAL THOUGHTS

LET'S TALK ABOUT SUICIDE.

Everyone seems to be talking about it.
It's all over the news, social media, and in our entertainment. It's almost as if suicide has become a fad. A trend. A meme.

MY EXPERIENCE

I was sexually abused repeatedly in childhood. There were multiple perpetrators.

Both grandfathers died early. I barely knew either of them.

I was a nerd at school. I dressed funny. I was small. I was bullied a lot.

My mom drifted into mental illness. She became delusional.

My parents separated and divorced. I lived with Mom.

Mom fell apart emotionally. I moved in with Dad.

Several months later, dad had a heart attack right in front of me. I watched him stop breathing.

At his funeral, I thought…

> *"If this is what life is like, I'm not sure I can make it."*

Mom moved back in after Dad's death. She attempted suicide soon after that.

What was going through my mind?

> *"Great. Just like I thought. I'm alone."*
> *"Everyone leaves. It's me against the world."*
> *"I'm not worth hanging around for."*
> *"You're willing to make me an orphan. I obviously don't matter."*
> *"There's no love here, or you wouldn't do this."*

What was Mom thinking?

I don't know. She never talked about it. I can only guess.

In the last several years, I have spoken at more than a dozen funerals of teens and others who took their own lives.

I have several friends who lost their son or daughter to suicide.

As a grief counselor, I've interacted with many grieving families and attempted to help them with the aftermath.

The sadness, confusion, and anger are intense. The guilt is devastating.

The ripple effects of suicide in the lives of parents, grandparents, siblings, and friends go on and on.

Hearts are crushed and shattered. The impact is incredibly destructive.

Those who take their own lives either knowingly or unknowingly thrust those who care about them into a suffocating cloud of pain.

> **If you're having suicidal thoughts, or have struggled with them in the past...**

Not every thought you have is yours.

Some thoughts that run through your head don't originate with you. They come from others. They come from messages you've been fed and believed along the way.

We're all influenced by the thoughts, words, and actions of those around us. We're impacted by what we're exposed to (or expose ourselves to). Influences seep in unevaluated through media, games, entertainment, peers, etc.

In other words, if you're having thoughts of harming yourself or taking your own life, you're probably buying into messages you're getting from the outside.

Are you going to let outside messages chart your course?

Are you going to give your heart over to negative and destructive influences?

You can't afford to do that. You were designed for difference-making.

Suicidal thoughts ultimately come from lies and limiting beliefs.

If you struggle with suicidal thoughts, chances are you've swallowed some lies. Those lies are now exerting their influence.

> *"I have nothing to look forward to."*
> *"It's all downhill from here."*
> *"It will always be this way."*
> *"The pain is too great."*
> *"I'm alone. No one cares."*

All of these, and any version of them, ultimately come from a larger lie.

> *"Now is forever."*

In other words, it will never get better. It'll only get worse. And there's an even larger lie lurking underneath that.

> *"There's no hope."*

Then, it becomes personalized.

> *"There's no hope <u>for me.</u>"*

SUICIDAL THOUGHTS COMING FROM LIES CAN BE REPLACED WITH THE TRUTH.

Now is not forever. Things change. People change. You can change. Healing and growth are change, and you can do both.

You're wired for connection with others. You're designed for impact. Hopeless, suicidal thoughts want to keep you from this.

Hope is always here. The problem is our eyesight. The lies we adhere to may blind us to hope, even if it's right in front of us.

As cliché as it may sound, there is truth in this; when hope has departed, you must remove the blindfold and see the hope in front of you to begin living again.

Sometimes our vision is off and the pain is so great that we have to search for hope. If we endure, we almost always find what we search for.

Hope is always with you.
You just need eyes to see it.
Most of the time, you'll need the
help of others to do this.

If you're wrestling with self-harming thoughts, by sure to read *Rachel's Story* in the back of this book just before the page titled *An Urgent Request*.

LIVING ON A DIFFERENT KIND OF EDGE

BEFORE WE SAID THAT THERE'S a difference between living on the edge of your seat and walking on the edge of a cliff.

It's time to exchange the edge of the cliff for the edge of your seat.

What does this mean? Sure, you can sit here and think in theoretical terms and metaphors, but without application, this is meaningless.

It means embracing who you really are and living that out.

Who are you?

You are a Difference-Maker.

Yep. You. You were made for this.

You have more influence that you know — an influence for good. You can have more impact on the world — positive, life-changing impact — than you dreamed possible.

Where does this begin?

It begins with two things:

1. Identifying and exposing the lies you've embraced.
2. Identifying, pursuing, and believing the Truth.

REPLACING LIES WITH THE TRUTH

If you believe the lie that "now is forever," begin replacing it with the truth.

> *"Now is not forever.*
> *I can heal and grow.*
> *Things can change."*

If hope seems to have disappeared, and your mind is drifting toward believing that it no longer exists for you, replace that lie with a liberating truth.

> *"Hope is always here.*
> *I will discover it over time."*

Lies about who you are...

Next comes facing the lies. These lies focus on your identity. Their goal is to deceive you about who you are.

> **LIE:**
> **"I'M WORTHLESS."**

Really? Who says?

You're one of a kind in human history. There has never been another exactly like you, and there never will be again.

You're unique. Your relationships are unique. Your life is unique. Unique. Special. Valuable.

This is true, apart from anything you've ever thought, said, or done. This is who you are.

> ***THE TRUTH:***
> *"I'M UNIQUE AND VALUABLE."*

Go ahead. Say it. Just speaking it out loud can have positive effects.

And if you're unique and valuable, you're significant. You matter. You're here for a reason. You have a mission – unique to you – that only you can live.

Whatever that mission is, it's about difference-making.

If you don't find that mission and live it, you miss out — and so do we.

> ***The Truth:***
> ***"I'm significant."***

Again, say it. Let yourself hear the words.

You're more important than you realize. Unique. Valuable. Significant.

On to another lie...

> **Lie:**
> **"I'm not enough."**

This is certainly a familiar one.

Not smart enough. Not attractive enough. Not good enough.

Not talented enough, strong enough, or rich enough.

Not enough.

Not enough for what? Not enough for whom?

No, you're not perfect. You never will be. Neither will anyone else.

"Not enough" usually comes from comparing yourself with others. Comparison is inherently associated with lies.

To compare is to lose. Why? Because we're all unique.

You're not perfect, but perfection isn't the goal. It can't be. It's impossible. Frankly, no one knows what perfection looks like or how to accomplish it. It's not objective. To chase perfection is to waste away chasing the wind.

You're imperfect. You're fallible. You make mistakes. This is part of being human.

So, what's the truth you need to embrace instead of the lie, "I'm not enough?"

How about this?

> ***THE TRUTH:***
> *"I'M IMPERFECT, AND THAT'S OKAY."*

Read that again.

Take a moment to truly reflect on it.

Speak it.

You're free to not be perfect, because you never will be.

You're free to become the difference-maker you were designed to be.

Embrace imperfection and use it as fuel to strive for something better.

> **LIE:**
> **"I'M ALONE."**

You may feel alone occasionally. Perhaps it's a constant feeling.

Are you alone?

No.

No one knows your thoughts or what's happening in your heart. But we all feel and think similar things in life. Each one of us is walking our own path.

However, life works much better when we walk together and support one another.

If you are isolating yourself or withdrawing from others, you may want to rethink this.

Retreating is something we all do when we're hurt. It's a natural self-preservation instinct and a comfortable coping mechanism. Yet, we also need to stay connected to other people. You're designed for connection. Life is ultimately about relationships. When you don't embrace and live this, you separate yourself from a lot of good.

You may feel alone. But this is far from the truth.

We're in this together. Thank goodness.

> ***The Truth:***
> *"I'm not alone. Period."*

Read it again. Think about it for a moment. Say it out loud. Let the truth sink in.

On to the next lie…

> **Lie:**
> *"I'm damaged."*

When we think we're damaged, what we're usually thinking – and believing – is that we're beyond repair.

Broken. Shattered. Crushed.

You've been wounded, perhaps deeply.

Maybe you feel like you're in a pit so deep that you can't possibly get out.

You may feel so bruised and broken that you believe that no one will ever love you for who you really are.

No one is beyond repair.

No one is beyond help and healing. No one.

Healing is real. It is possible.

No, you are not damaged beyond all hope. Yes, you can heal.

Healing takes guts. You have to make the choice to heal.

You must believe healing is out there, break free of the lies, and pursue helpful people and relationships.

THE TRUTH:
"I'VE BEEN WOUNDED, BUT I CAN HEAL."

Read this one slowly.

Say it out loud.

Take a deep breath and repeat it.

Tell yourself the truth.

LIE:
"I'M INVISIBLE."

You might think, "No one notices me. They don't even know I'm here."

Or maybe, "I just wear a mask. No one knows the real me. I'm invisible."

It's true that no one knows the real you perfectly. Neither do you. People create their idea of you based on what you reveal to and share with them.

It's your choice to share. It's their choice to listen and accept you, or not.

The truth is we all want to be seen. All of us. That's part of the reason why we do the crazy, attention-getting stuff we do.

I've discovered in life that as I take time to see other people, some of them take the time to see who I am.

Try it. Look at the world and people around you. Train yourself to see the person in front of you. Get out of your own head for a while and enter their world.

Watch what happens.

Let's restructure this limiting lie into an active truth.

> **THE TRUTH:**
> *"I MIGHT FEEL INVISIBLE, BUT IF I SEEK TO SEE OTHERS, I'LL BE SEEN IN RETURN."*

Read that again. Take a moment to reflect on its meaning.

What would it look like for you to see others?

You won't been seen by everyone, no. Some people are so absorbed in their own world that they haven't discovered how to see others yet. That is out of your control.

But there are people out there living outside of themselves. They look to connect and relate. They listen. They care. They will see you.

These are the people you want to find and spend time with.

> **THE TRUTH:**
> *"AS I SEE OTHERS, I WILL BE SEEN BY THOSE WHO WANT TO SEE ME."*

Take a look at that truth again. Read it out loud.

> **LIE:**
> *"I'M UGLY."*

Our world is obsessed with appearances. Our media is permeated by what's attractive and sexy. We're aware of this and constantly compare ourselves with it.

Recall our previous discussion about when we compare, we lose. Every time. This is where this pattern often shows itself.

Consciously or subconsciously, you compare yourself with others. Your view of yourself is mostly appearance-oriented, based on someone else's definition of attractiveness.

Frankly, this is terrible.

Of course, perhaps you see this, are angry about it, and have gone the other way. You could care less what you look like. You know you can't win the game, so you quit trying.

Yet, you still look in the mirror and sigh.

Let's be realistic. The standards of attractiveness most of us hold are based on carefully posed, enhanced, photoshopped images in near perfect environments.

In other words, our definitions of what's beautiful and handsome are based on altered, doctored images. The people are real, but our concept of them is not.

Plain and simple, our societal ideas of beauty are often lies.

The next time you look in the mirror, try to recognize the truth.

Valuable. Special. Imperfect, but significant. Wounded, but repairable.

What's the truth?

> ### THE TRUTH:
> ### "I'M MORE THAN MY APPEARANCE!"

You are not your appearance. You are far, far more than this.

WHAT WILL YOU DO WITH THESE LIES?

These are not all the lies out there, of course. They are many more. Many of them, however, are simply other versions of the lies we've already discussed.

Look into your own heart. I have some questions for you.

What lies have you believed?

Are you willing to see them for what they are — lies?

Are you willing to learn to replace these lies with the truth?

Seriously consider these questions.

What are your answers?

Perhaps you can sense the change coming. Yes, this is going to take some effort.

You may be reading this and asking yourself, "Why is this guy asking me all this?

Why did he write this book anyway?"

I'm writing this because I believe something very strongly.

I believe you are a Difference-Maker.

I also believe that you will live out what you really believe about yourself.

Our world desperately needs Difference-Makers who are living their mission. Our world needs you.

Yes, you.

And yes, I believe this with all my heart.

Don't cheat yourself, and don't cheat us.

You might see yourself as a mere caterpillar right now, but you have the DNA of a butterfly.

Believe it, and begin to think and act like it's true.

THE FOUR-STEP CHALLENGE

Here's my challenge.

TAKE THESE FOUR STEPS:

"Look Out Lies. I'm Coming for You!"

1. Identify your lies.

Expose them. Write them down and get familiar with them.

If you do this, you'll be able to recognize them when they appear.

Try writing some of them down here:

_____
_____
_____
_____
_____
_____
_____
_____
_____
_____

"The Truth is Out There, and I'm Going to Find It!"

2. Know and embrace the truth.

Look at the lies you wrote down above.

From each lie, ask yourself, "What's the truth?"

Write these truths down.

Read them over, slowly.

Though some truths might seem too good to be true, take them in.

Picture yourself receiving them and taking them into your mind and heart.

You might want to write these truths — and the lies you listed — on a piece of paper or enter them in a note on your computer.

Post it where you will see it every day.

Read them often. Remind yourself.

Immerse yourself in these truths.

"Bye, Bye, Lies. Hello Truth!"

3. Put the lies in your rearview mirror and focus on the truths.

Your mind is the key. Your thoughts are the battleground of this fight.

If you want to be the Difference-Maker you were meant to be, *you must change the way you think.*

Intentionally fill your mind with truths. Read them daily — several times. Post them in places where you will see them. Get creative about surrounding yourself with reminders to dwell in truth.

The more you gaze through the windshield at truth, the more

you'll move forward, and the more fulfilling and rewarding your journey will be.

If you spend too much time looking in the rearview mirror, however, you're inviting pain and disaster.

Glance in the rearview mirror.

Be aware of the lies behind you.

Gaze through the windshield.

Focus on the truths around you.

Know the truth. Believe it. Begin acting like it's true.

"I Won't Go it Alone. I Can't!"

4. Intentionally include others in your difference-making journey.

Here's a key principle for a healthy and productive life:

Get around people who inspire and encourage you,

and limit your exposure to those who don't.

Someone once said that we become a composite of the five people we're around the most. Association has impact. You're profoundly influenced by who you spend time with – more than you know.

Who do you want to be? What kind of difference do you want to make?

Dream a little. Don't go all delusional, but push the envelope a bit on what you think is possible for you.

What kind of Difference-Maker do you want to be?

Now, consider this.

---
*Who can inspire and encourage you in
your journey toward becoming that?*

Whoever doesn't inspire you will usually drag you down. You can't afford that. The world can't afford that.

Find people — other Difference-Makers — who can walk with you the direction you are going.

Remember that exposing lies, believing the truth, and becoming a Difference-Maker is a journey. It happens over time.

Be patient with yourself. Be patient with others. We're all imperfect. We all stumble, and sometimes fall. The key is getting up as quickly as possible, learning what you can from the experience, and then moving forward.

YOU'RE ON YOUR WAY.

Don't stop here.

If you're interested in taking the Difference-Maker journey with me, check out my book:

***Difference Maker: Overcoming Adversity and
Turning Pain into Purpose, Every Day.***
https://www.garyroe.com/difference-maker

We're in this together. Let's do it.

ONE LAST THING:

IF SELF-DAMAGING OR SUICIDAL THOUGHTS come knocking… Involve someone else in what you're thinking and feeling. Share with someone you trust. Get it out in the open.

When we share what's happening inside us, something happens. Pressure gets released. Another person now knows, and still cares.

There is hope. Things can change.

As long as you have suicidal thoughts, keep sharing them. Peers are supportive, but you really need to involve an adult in this. Find one you can trust — or are willing to take a risk to trust – and share.

Get it out. Keep getting it out.

Lies have far more power when they are secret. They take on a life of their own. Don't let them determine or drive your life.

Yes, you might feel ashamed or embarrassed. You might be terrified of sharing what you're thinking. That's natural.

Fear and shame want to keep you stuck. They want to take over. They want to keep you in the downward spiral of secret thoughts.

You are not what you feel. You are not the shame you experience. Fear and shame are barriers to healing and growth.

Be courageous.

Share.

When you're real with someone else about what's going on inside you, you open yourself up to good things.

> **If self-harming thoughts invade,
> who are you going to contact?
> Parent? Coach? Teacher?
> Counselor? Mentor? Friend?
> Suicide hotline?**
> 1-800-273-8255
> **Crisis Text Line: text HOME to 741741
> Decide now. Be prepared.**

RACHEL'S STORY

I STRUGGLED WITH SUICIDAL THOUGHTS FROM the age of 7. That was the first time I remember really thinking about it.

I was terribly sensitive to little hurts, and of course big ones too. The hurts piled up over the years. The pain got to be too much. I started to numb myself out. Life became a constant battle between feeling the pain and running from it. Honestly, my teen years were pretty miserable at times.

Thoughts of harming myself came. Sometimes it was a sharp, impulsive feeling in difficult moments where I just felt like I needed to escape and cut off the pain. Other times it was a dull, constant state of being I would fade into of simply wanting "to go home" – as if I knew my spirit was much more than this body and I didn't see the "point" in living through all this pain. I didn't know how to "access" my feelings of love even with my family or boyfriend at the time, who all tried their best to support me through love, counseling, and even trials with medication.

In the end, I had to summon the strength within me to explore the possibility of there being another way to live that didn't seem so scary or painful. It was a lot to work through and heal within myself. It required a lot of self-compassion and self-forgiveness. Now I can't imagine abandoning myself that way, especially in my darker moments. But I didn't have those tools at the time, so I understand why that option "made sense" to my fearful mind.

When I learned how to face those scary feelings, rather than numbing out, trusting love to pull me through (which it always,

always does), then things slowly but truly turned around. I think we all as human beings can forget how to access that feeling of love within us, versus just having it as an intellectual concept in our heads. But especially for a child or teenager, the world is still too foreign and unknown. I lived in a place of disconnection and fear, which only amplified the voice inside that me that suicide is a better alternative.

I can only imagine how much grief there is to sort through when everyone who is left behind has to try and understand why someone would choose to leave all those who loved them. I know it is such a sore but important topic for many of us. Finding help in those teen years feels almost impossible at times. Your thoughts can trick you into thinking you don't want help or support – that you want to remain isolated. I can't help but feel that if we can talk about suicide prevention more in our society, without the extremes of shame or glamorizing it, then hopefully down the road a bit the numbers of suicidal teens will be decreasing, not increasing.

There is always hope. Life was so hard and painful at times, but I held on. Hope was there all the time. I just didn't have eyes to see it sometimes.

AN URGENT REQUEST

(CAN YOU HELP ME OUT?)

One last thing…

If you found **Living on the Edge** helpful, I need your help.

Could you help me reach others who need this message?

You can be a Difference Maker by writing a simple review of this book and posting it on the site where the book was purchased. You might need to use a parent's account to do this.

Just answer this question.

How did this book affect you?

Make it short and sweet, 1-3 sentences.

I read these reviews. They help me be a better writer, and to become even more of the Difference-Maker I was designed to be.

Your review helps us reach more people. It's a small thing, but it can make a big impact.

Thanks for your help!

ABOUT THE AUTHOR

Hi. My name is Gary.

My background wasn't the best. I was repeatedly sexually abused in childhood by multiple people. I was bullied at school. My grandfathers died before I really knew them. One of my good friends died of an illness in 7th grade. My mom struggled with mental illness and attempted suicide. My parents divorced. My dad died suddenly. I was basically orphaned at 15.

I was a competitive swimmer growing up. This ended up saving my life. It kept me busy, healthy, and controlled my anxiety. A family I knew well from swim team took me in. Their love and acceptance changed the course of my life.

I set out on a journey to heal and grow. I finished high school and went on to study Psychology in college. I then headed to Seminary and got two Masters' degrees, one in Biblical Studies and the other in Theology and Leadership. I served as a college minister, and then went to Japan as a missionary. After a number of years, I came back to the United States and served as a pastor of several churches in Texas and Washington. I now work as an author, speaker, hospice chaplain, and grief counselor. I've written 12 books so far and have more than 600 articles to my credit.

My adult life has been about helping hurting people heal and grow. Part of this is challenging myself and them to turn the bad stuff into good stuff and be the Difference-Makers they were designed to be. Most days, I'm in awe. I can't believe I get to do this. I'm grateful.

None of this is about me. I am where I am because of those who've gone before me. I stand on their shoulders. I have done nothing but receive, and then use what I've been given for good.

I'm married to an amazing woman named Jen. She's my hero. She's been through more than you can imagine and come out on the other side. She's a Difference-Maker, and she makes my life better each day.

I have seven adopted kids. They're an amazing crew. I still have two teens at home. They keep me laughing, scratching my head, and growing. I have two grandkids, so far. Life is busy. I like puns (especially the bad ones), working-out, wild Hawaiian shirts, hockey, and tofu. I live in Texas.

I'm on the Difference-Maker journey with you. I'm still learning, every day.

Visit me at www.garyroe.com. Email me. I would be honored to "meet" you.

KEEP GOING!

YOU'RE ON YOUR WAY.

Don't stop here.

If you're interested in taking the Difference-Maker journey with me, check out my book:

> ***Difference Maker: Overcoming Adversity and***
> ***Turning Pain into Purpose, Every Day.***
> https://www.garyroe.com/difference-maker

We're in this together. It's time to make a difference.

www.ingramcontent.com/pod-product-compliance
Lightning Source LLC
Chambersburg PA
CBHW030104100526
44591CB00008B/271